THE STORY OF THOMAS JEFFERSON

A Biography Book for New Readers

Written by
Lisa Trusiani

Illustrated by
Patrick Corrigan

ROCKRIDGE PRESS

Dedicated to equal and impartial
Justice under the law
and
the Truth, may it continue
to set people free.

For general information on our other products and services or to obtain technical support, please contact our Customer Care Department within the United States at (866) 744-2665, or outside the United States at (510) 253-0500.

Rockridge Press publishes its books in a variety of electronic and print formats. Some content that appears in print may not be available in electronic books, and vice versa.

Series Designer: Angela Navarra
Interior and Cover Designers: Liz Cosgrove and Lindsey Dekker
Art Producer: Hannah Dickerson Editor: Kristen Depken
Production Editor: Mia Moran

ISBN: Print 978-1-64739-833-0 | eBook 978-1-64739-530-8
R0

Printed in China

CONTENTS

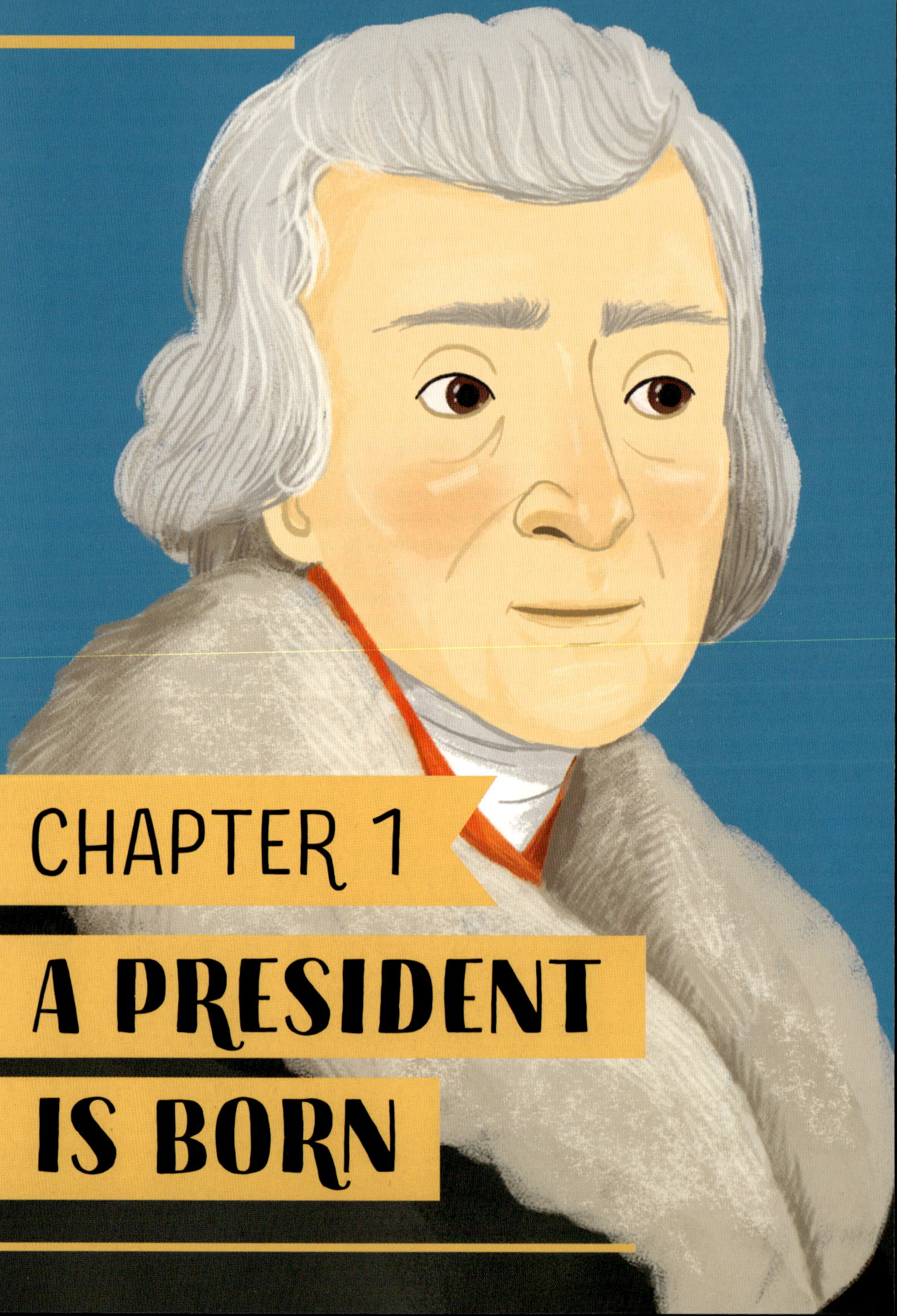

CHAPTER 1
A PRESIDENT IS BORN

Meet Thomas Jefferson

When Thomas Jefferson was five years old, he had read every book in his house. His father had more than 20 books, a large library to have at home in the 1700s. Thomas believed books were **precious**.

Books told Thomas stories. Some helped him learn math and history. When Thomas was a teenager, he read books by great thinkers. Thomas was always thinking about new ideas. The more Thomas read, the sharper his own ideas became.

When Thomas grew up, his ideas changed the world. He put them into the **Declaration of Independence** and helped create the United States of America. Thomas became the third **president** of the United States, and his idea to buy land from the Mississippi River to the Rocky Mountains made the United States twice as large. When his job as president ended,

Thomas had the idea to create a public **university**, and he did.

This is the story of Thomas Jefferson and how he helped the United States grow into the country it is today.

Thomas's World

Thomas Jefferson was born April 13, 1743, on Shadwell Plantation, his family's farm in Virginia. He and his two older sisters lived with their parents, Jane Randolph Jefferson and Peter Jefferson, in a wooden house near the Rivanna River. Thomas was the third of their 10 children. Their farm was 1,200 **acres**, almost two square miles. Large farms in Virginia were called **plantations**, and the owners were **planters**.

JUMP IN THE THINK TANK

What are some of your favorite books? What do you like about them?

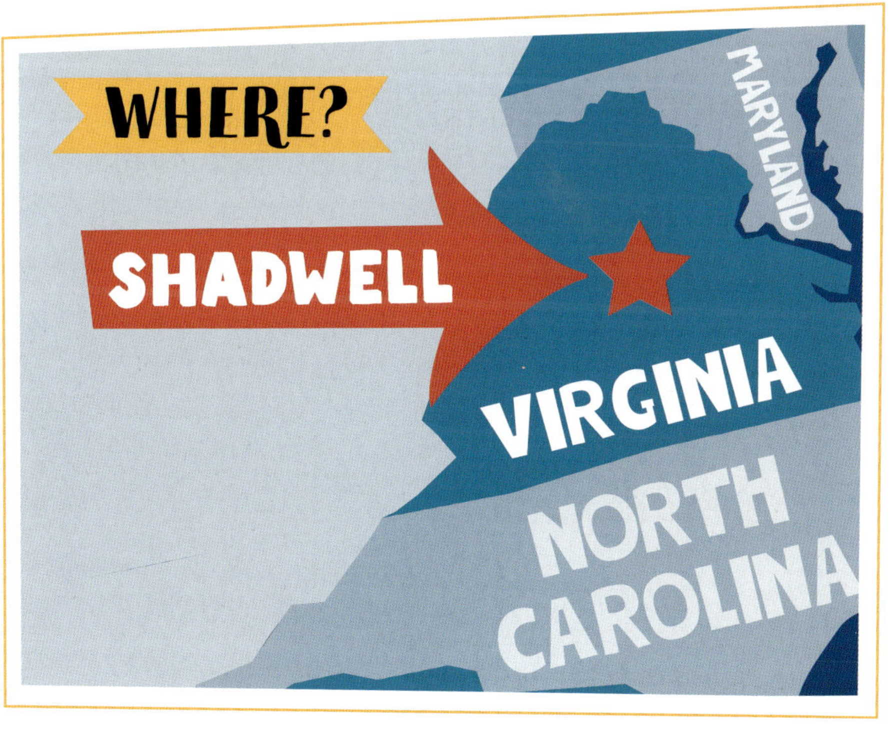

Like many people living in Virginia, Thomas's mother had been born in England. Peter and Jane did not come from very **wealthy** families. Their fathers were considered gentlemen, or well respected men, who eventually gained wealth. They soon had more money, property, and power than most people in Virginia.

MYTH & FACT

Myth: Thomas never played outside. He only read books.

Fact: Thomas liked to play outside. A favorite place was a little mountain on his family's plantation.

Today, Virginia is a state, one of 50 states in the United States of America. When Thomas was born, Virginia was a **colony**, one of 13 American colonies. England owned the colonies, and the king of England ruled everyone who lived there. A person born in Virginia was an English **citizen**, even if they never set foot in England.

WHEN?

1736 Peter Jefferson buys 1,200 acres in Virginia.

1739 Jane Randolph and Peter Jefferson marry.

1743 Thomas Jefferson is born in Virginia.

CHAPTER 2

THE EARLY YEARS

Life in Virginia

Thomas was two years old when his family moved 50 miles away to Tuckahoe Plantation to live with Thomas's young cousins whose parents had died. For seven years, they all lived together. **Tutors** taught Thomas reading, writing, and math. In the evening, Thomas and his father talked about books. Peter also taught Thomas to ride a horse, hunt, and fish.

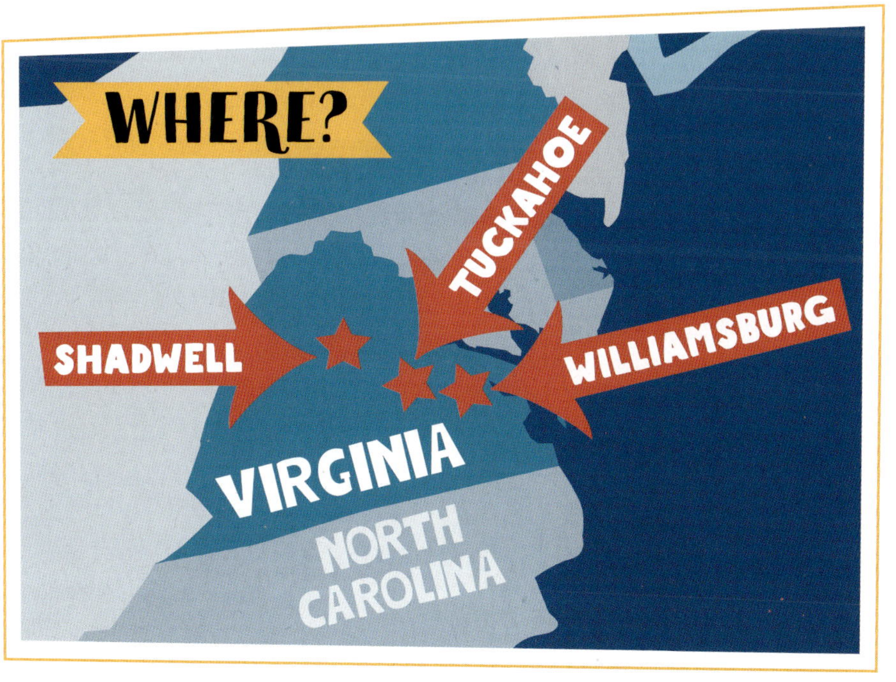

Thomas liked being with his father, but Peter was often away. He traveled between Tuckahoe and his own plantation, Shadwell. He also worked as a **surveyor**, exploring land where **native** people, not **colonists**, lived. Thomas's father drew maps and wrote reports about the trees, water, animals, and people there.

Sometimes Thomas went with his father to check on his property. His father had large fields of crops, but he didn't take care of them himself.

Planters forced **enslaved people**, called **slaves**, to clear fields, plant seeds, and then tend and pick the crops. Paying for this hard work would have cost a lot of money, but the enslaved people were not paid. They were not free to leave, stop working, or live with their own families. Early on, most enslaved people in the colonies were Native American. Later, most were **African** or African American.

JUMP IN THE THINK TANK

Imagine being forced to live without your family, and to do hard physical work every day instead of going to school. How do you think you would feel?

MYTH & FACT

MYTH: All slaves worked in the fields.

FACT: Enslaved people also cared for the planters' families. Thomas said his first memory was being carried on a horse by an enslaved man.

When Thomas was born, **slavery** was legal in all 13 colonies, even though it was cruel and wrong.

Study Time

When Thomas was nine years old, his family moved back to Shadwell Plantation, and Thomas went to boarding school 50 miles away.

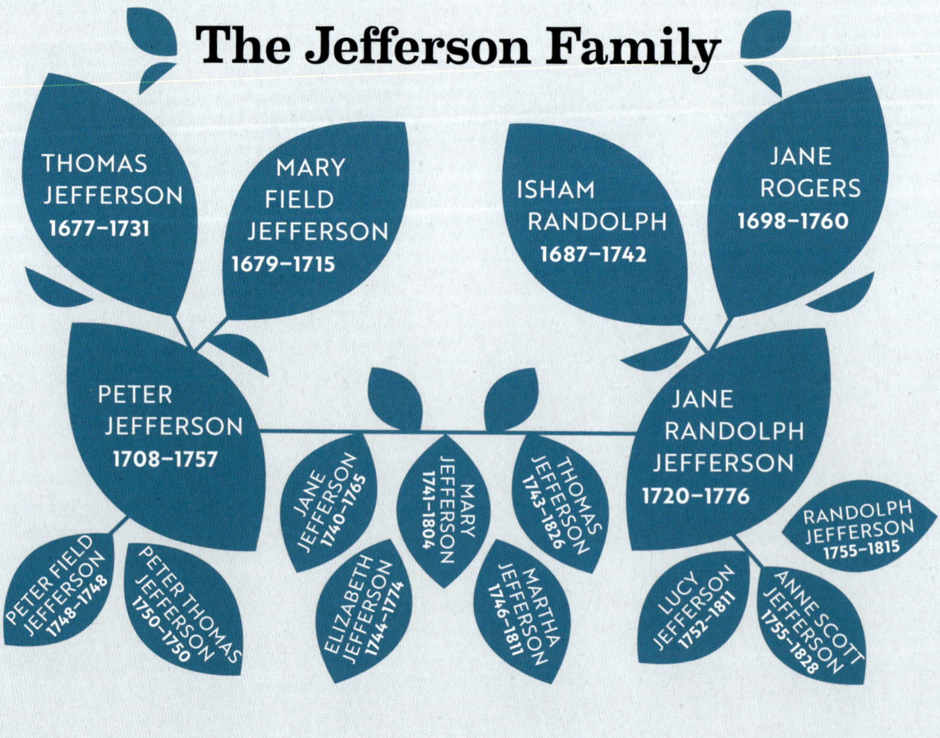

He learned to play the violin and to read Greek, Latin, and French.

When Thomas was 14 years old, his father fell ill and died. Thomas was heartbroken. He knew his father wanted him to go to **college**, so Thomas focused on his studies and went to the College of William & Mary in Williamsburg, Virginia. At the time, William & Mary was only for men who were white and wealthy.

Thomas read books and poems that were thousands of years old. He played violin for three hours a day. Thomas worked very hard at his studies. He also met many smart people with important jobs. One friend was a **lawyer**. When Thomas finished college, he knew he wanted to be a lawyer, too.

WHEN?

1745
The Jefferson family moves to Tuckahoe.

1752
The Jefferson family returns to Shadwell.

1752
Thomas leaves for boarding school.

1757
Peter Jefferson dies.

1762
Thomas finishes college.

CHAPTER 3

THOMAS THE LAWYER

A New Career

When Thomas decided to become a lawyer, he didn't go to law school—there weren't any in the colonies. Instead law students worked for lawyers who trained them. Thomas worked for his friend George Wythe. Thomas liked the work, and he liked George, who made Thomas study very hard. Thomas stayed for five years, much longer than most students, because he was learning so much. George was like a walking, talking law library. Thomas didn't want to leave!

MYTH & FACT

MYTH	FACT
Thomas was a great public speaker.	Thomas did not like to give speeches, but he was a great writer.

When Thomas passed the law test and became a lawyer, he was busy right away. Thomas had many clients and more than 100 cases a year. Most clients were white, but a few were enslaved African Americans.

Thomas wanted to help make laws, too. In Virginia, men who owned land could **vote** for leaders to **represent** them and make laws. They voted for Thomas. He became part of a group of **representatives** called the **House of Burgesses**. They met in Williamsburg. Though Thomas spoke in a quiet way, the words he wrote were powerful. He became famous in the House for a booklet he wrote that declared England had no right to rule the American colonies.

Monticello

When his father died, Thomas **inherited** his books and Shadwell Plantation. There were miles of land, a large house, and dozens of enslaved people. Thomas took charge of Shadwell when he was 21 years old. Until then, his mother had been in charge.

Thomas liked **architecture**. He drew plans for a new home with a round roof and giant columns. He named it Monticello, which means "little mountain" in Italian. He wanted to live on the high hill where he had played as a child. When he was ready to start **construction**, enslaved people chopped down trees and built a

simple, one-room building that they would one day rebuild into a mansion.

At the time, Thomas was living at Shadwell Plantation in the house where he had been born. He was happy there, and it was easy to travel to work. One day, while Thomas was visiting a neighbor, the Shadwell house burned down.

JUMP IN THE THINK TANK

When Shadwell Plantation burned, Thomas was sad to lose his papers and books. What are your most precious belongings?

No one was hurt, but the fire destroyed Thomas's precious books.

With the Shadwell house gone, Thomas moved to Monticello. Around this time, he also met Martha Wayles Skelton, a wealthy 22-year-old widow. Martha played the piano, and Thomas played the violin. They played songs together and fell in love. In 1772, Thomas and Martha got married and soon

had a baby girl. They named her Martha and called her Patsy.

Thomas was very happy, but England was beginning to cause trouble. They had added new, unfair **taxes** to things the colonists bought. The colonists, including Thomas, did not want to pay. It was time for action.

WHEN?

1762	Thomas begins to study law with George Wythe.
1767	Thomas becomes a lawyer in Virginia.
1769	Thomas is **elected** to the House of Burgesses.
1769	Construction begins on Monticello.
1770	Shadwell burns down; Thomas moves to Monticello.
1772	Thomas and Martha marry and have their first child.

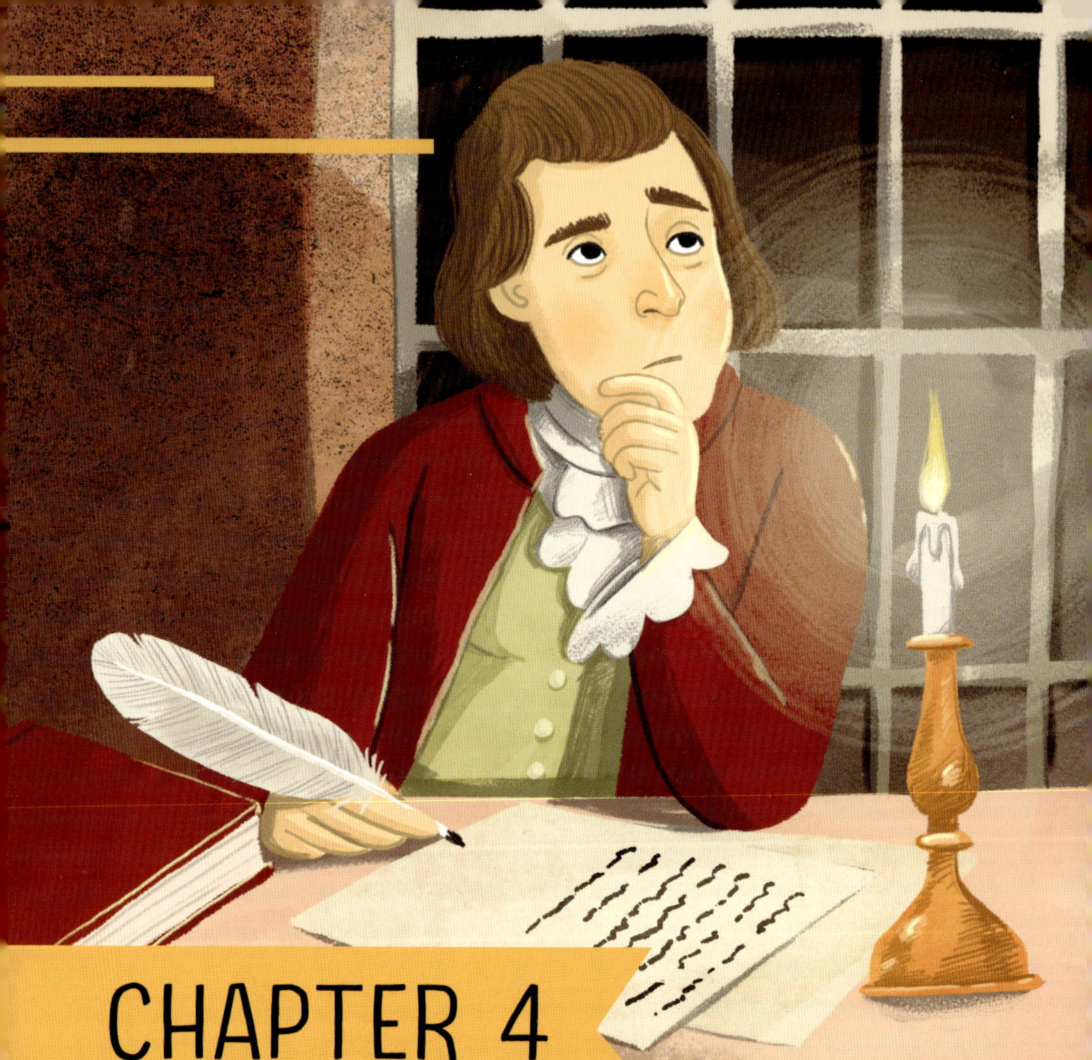

CHAPTER 4

A REVOLUTIONARY LEADER

Time for Action

At the House of Burgesses, Thomas and the other representatives talked about England's new taxes, including a tax on tea, a very popular drink. Thomas believed the colonists should not be taxed because they could not **elect** anyone to represent them in England's **government**.

In Massachusetts, colonists went onto English ships and dumped their tea into Boston Harbor. It was a tax **protest**. Today it is called the Boston Tea Party. England punished Massachusetts. They shut down Boston Harbor. No supplies came in. No goods to sell went out.

MYTH & FACT

MYTH: Thomas went to Boston to take part in the Boston Tea Party protest.

FACT: Thomas was in Virginia that night. He later planned a protest that took place in Virginia on the day England shut down Boston Harbor.

Thomas convinced the House of Burgesses to protest by refusing to work. This made England angry, and it shut down the House. The representatives met secretly and planned a meeting with **delegates** from other colonies. This was called a **congress**.

The congress was held in Philadelphia in 1774. The delegates discussed whether to stay with England or break away. Thomas was ill and couldn't go, so he sent the booklet he had written. It said the colonies were states, and

England had no right to rule them. Not everyone was ready for Thomas's **revolutionary** ideas.

A year later, at the **Second Continental Congress** in Philadelphia, more delegates were ready. There had been bloody battles between English soldiers and colonists in Massachusetts. Leaders asked Thomas to write a document, using his ideas to tell the world England did not rule the 13 American states.

The Declaration of Independence

Thomas worried he wouldn't do a good job on this important document. But when others said he should be the one to write it, Thomas set up a desk in a room across the street from the congress.

Thomas dipped the end of his **quill** pen into ink and began to write the Declaration of Independence. Thomas said the colonies were now states, and they had joined together to become the United States of America. It would be a **democracy**, and England had no right to rule them. Thomas wrote that all men were created equal and ruled themselves. The government would protect their **rights** to live, to be free, and to choose how they lived their lives. When the Declaration was written, these rights did not extend to enslaved people, **indigenous** people, or women. Today, African Americans, **Native Americans**, and women have gained important rights, but the fight for **equality** continues.

JUMP IN THE THINK TANK

Thomas wrote most of the Declaration of Independence, but other people added ideas, too. When you have a project, do you like working with other people?

Thomas showed the Declaration to other delegates, who made some changes. Thomas didn't like all the changes, but he included most of them. By July 4, 1776, the congress agreed to the final wording of the Declaration of Independence. They voted to break away from England and create a new nation.

Thomas and the other delegates sent the Declaration to the king. They knew England would not let the colonies go without a fight. So the congress voted for George Washington to build and lead an army. Soon after reading the Declaration, England sent warships and thousands of soldiers. They wanted to win the **Revolutionary War**.

WHEN?

1773	The Boston Tea Party takes place.
1774	England shuts down the House of Burgesses.
1774	A congress is held in Philadelphia.
1775	The Second Continental Congress begins.
1776	The Declaration of Independence is written.

CHAPTER 5

A TIME OF CHANGE

Back to Virginia

In 1776, Thomas was elected to the House of Delegates, the new government of the new state of Virginia. For three years, Thomas wrote new state laws to replace Virginia's old **colonial** laws. Some laws were about slavery. Thomas and the other delegates could have created new laws that ended slavery, but they did not. Slavery stayed legal in the state of Virginia, even though it was wrong. Thomas decided instead to fight for **freedom** of religion. The old law forced colonists to follow the king's religion. Thomas's new law allowed people to follow their **conscience**, to believe in a god or not, and to **practice** any religion or none.

Thomas was elected **governor** of Virginia in 1779. The United States and England were still at war. Thomas moved the **capital** from Williamsburg to Richmond, away from the river and enemy ships. He got the Virginia **militia** ready to fight.

From the end of December 1780 to January 1781, the British military attacked Virginia with English warships and more than 1,000 English soldiers. They burned most of Richmond and the towns nearby. Thomas ordered the Virginia militia to attack. They pushed the soldiers away.

JUMP —IN THE— THINK TANK

Can you think of a time when you listened to your conscience? What did it tell you to do?

A Dangerous Role

One day in June 1781, Thomas waited at Monticello. His term as governor was ending soon, and he had a meeting the next day in nearby Charlottesville. Virginia planned to elect a new governor, who would start the job right away.

> "Conscience is as much a part of a man as his leg or arm."

The same day, the **Green Dragoons** were heading to Monticello. They were fighters on horseback who had spent the war riding through Virginia destroying property. Some were English, and others were Americans who wanted England to win. They rode toward Monticello to capture Thomas. They planned to arrest him for **treason** and put him in prison.

As the Green Dragoons thundered past the Cuckoo Tavern on horseback, they did not see Jack Jouett, a member of the Virginia militia.

Jack saw them and guessed their plan. He jumped on his horse and rode all night through thick woods to avoid being seen. He didn't stop until he reached Monticello and warned Thomas. Thomas and his family escaped to another plantation they owned. At Monticello, an enslaved **butler** named Martin Hemings bravely told the Green Dragoons he did not know where Thomas was. The Dragoons rode away without destroying any property.

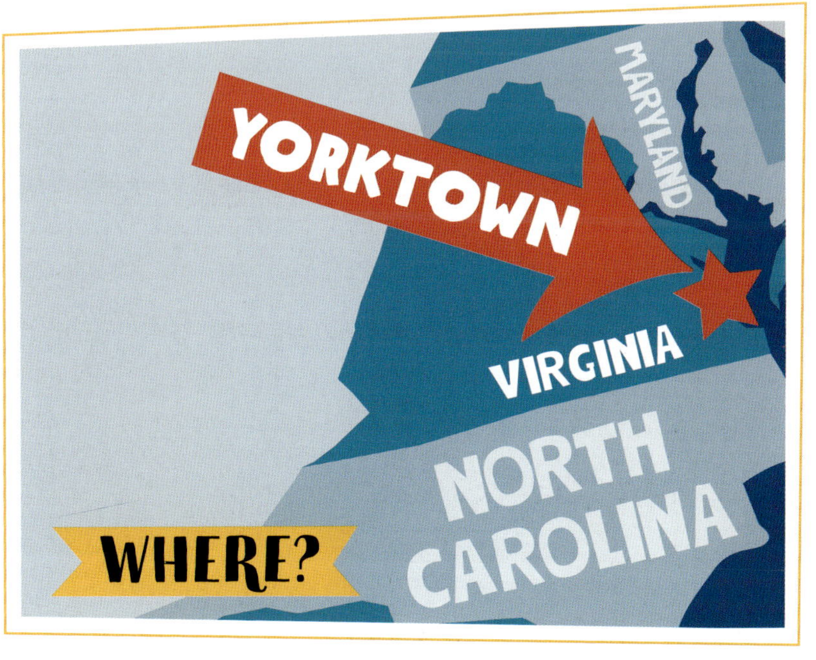

A few months later, George Washington's army defeated the English at Yorktown, Virginia. The French navy helped. Thomas knew that winning the Battle of Yorktown meant the United States would win the war.

WHEN?

1776	1779	1781
Thomas is elected to the Virginia House of Delegates.	Thomas becomes governor of Virginia.	The United States wins the Battle of Yorktown, Virginia.

CHAPTER 6
IMPORTANT JOBS

Thomas in France

Thomas and Martha were married for 10 years, and they loved each other deeply. Thomas was heartbroken when Martha died months after giving birth to their sixth child. Thomas's friends said he might feel better if he worked in government again. In 1783, Thomas was elected to the United States **Congress**. He was sent as an **ambassador** to France to make deals with other countries.

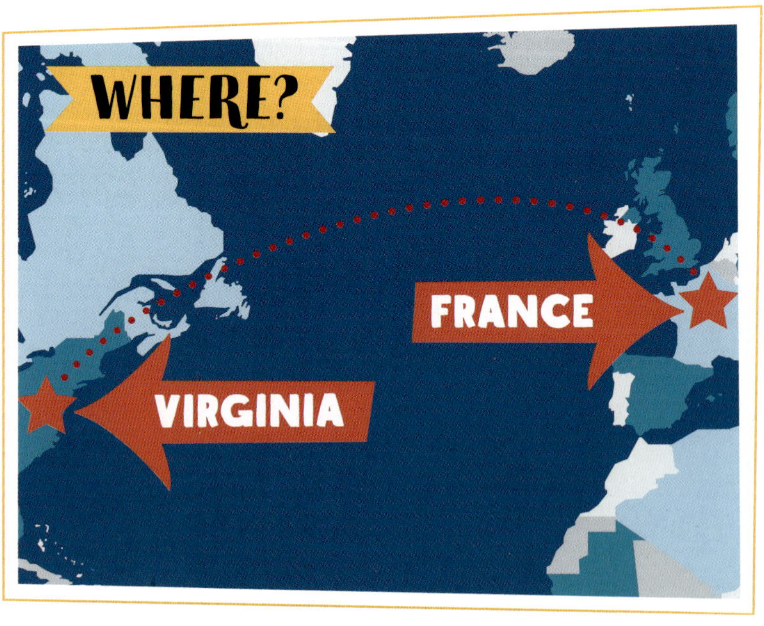

Thomas went to France with his oldest daughter, Patsy. Two years later, his daughter Polly joined them. A 14-year-old enslaved girl, Sally Hemings, traveled with Polly. Sally was related to Thomas's wife, Martha, because they had the same father. After Sally and Polly arrived, Polly went to school with Patsy, and Sally worked in Thomas's house.

Thomas searched for new ideas in France. He looked at the designs of buildings and gardens.

MYTH & FACT

MYTH: Thomas did not like France and was happy to go home to the United States.

FACT: Thomas liked France. He wanted to return to Paris, but he took the job as Secretary of State instead.

He bought 2,000 books for his home library. While Thomas was **fascinated** by French ideas, people in France were fascinated by Thomas's ideas. Some wanted a new government like the one forming in the United States. Thomas helped them write a document like the Declaration of Independence. He hoped the French people would break free from their king.

After five years, Thomas went home with his family.

Thomas in the Capital

While Thomas was in France, George Washington had been elected the first president of the United States. He asked Thomas to be Secretary of State. This meant he would decide how the United States should act toward other countries. He was in the president's **cabinet**, a group that helps the president make decisions. Another member was Alexander Hamilton. The two men had strong ideas. They argued in cabinet meetings, in Congress, and in the newspapers.

JUMP —IN THE— THINK TANK

Why do you think Thomas wanted to beat John Adams and become president of the United States?

Thomas's ideas kept the new country out of wars. But Thomas got tired of arguing with Alexander and resigned in 1793. He had ideas for big changes at Monticello. He designed a new house, then had enslaved people tear down his old house and build the new one. They also built a dairy, smokehouse, nail factory, and row of small cabins.

Thomas designed a better plow and clock and had them built. He played games with his grandchildren, and he had more children with Sally Hemings, the enslaved girl who had traveled to France with the Jefferson family.

In 1796, Thomas ran for president. John Adams won the most votes and became president. Thomas won the next highest number and became **vice president**. John and Thomas had been friends for years, but they had very different ideas. At first John listened to Thomas's ideas, but he soon stopped. Thomas did not like being ignored. In 1800, Thomas decided to run for president again. He wanted to beat John Adams, and he was certain he would win.

WHEN?

Thomas's wife, Martha, dies.

1782

Thomas becomes ambassador to France.

1784

Thomas returns to the United States.

1789

Thomas becomes Secretary of State.

1790

Thomas is elected vice president.

1797

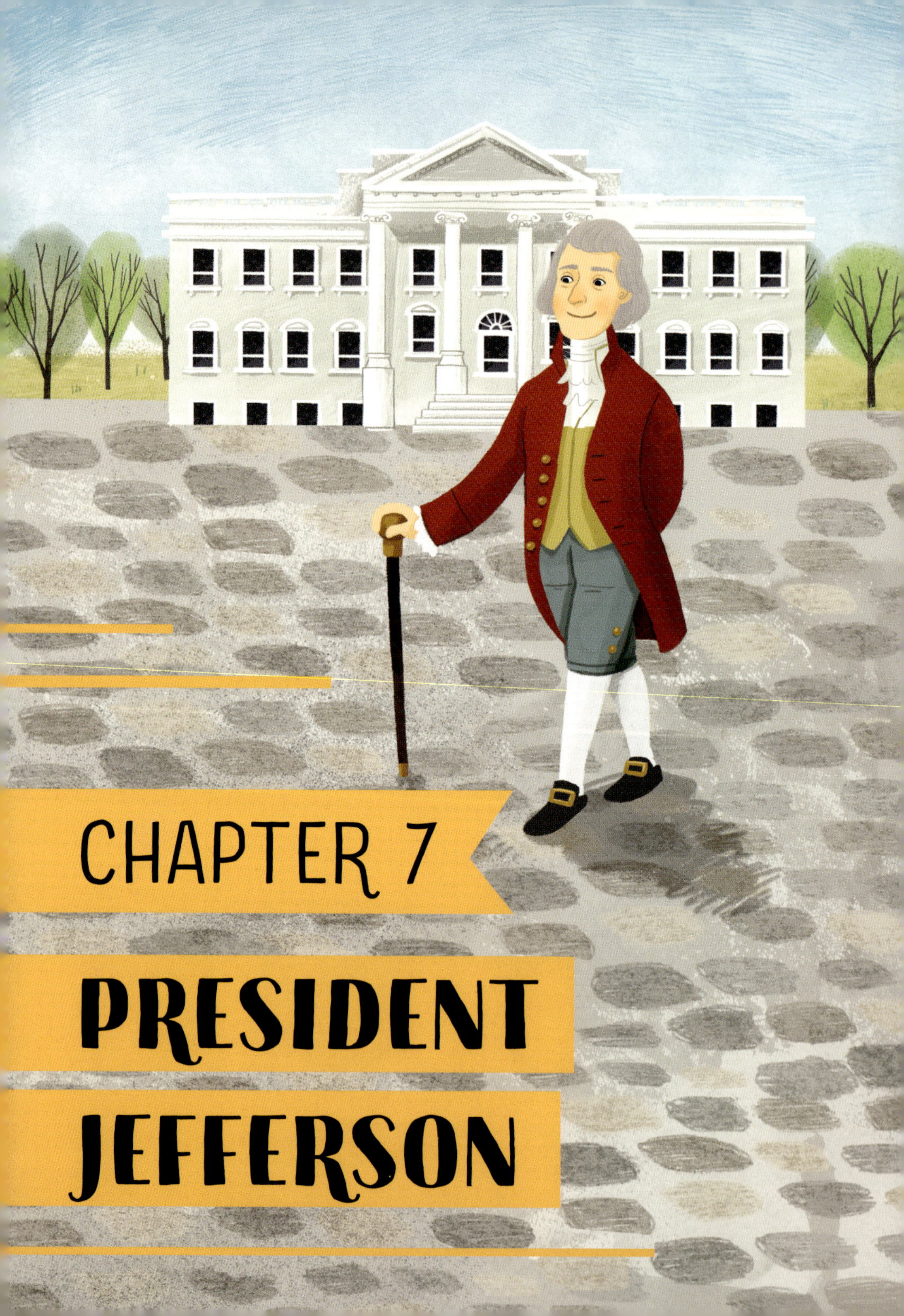

CHAPTER 7

PRESIDENT JEFFERSON

A Popular President

Becoming the third president of the United States was not as easy as Thomas had expected, but he won the **election** in 1801. Thomas did not want a president to act like a king, so he tried to live in a simple way. Thomas wanted the government to be simpler, too. He made the army and navy smaller and closed some government offices.

Thomas had an idea that changed the future of the United States. France owned the land from the Mississippi River to the Rocky Mountains. Thomas wanted the United States to buy it so that farmers could have more land and more power. The deal was called the Louisiana Purchase, and it doubled the size of the United States.

Indigenous people were living on this land already. Their **ancestors** had lived there for thousands of years. Thomas knew that many would probably be forced to leave. He made the deal anyway.

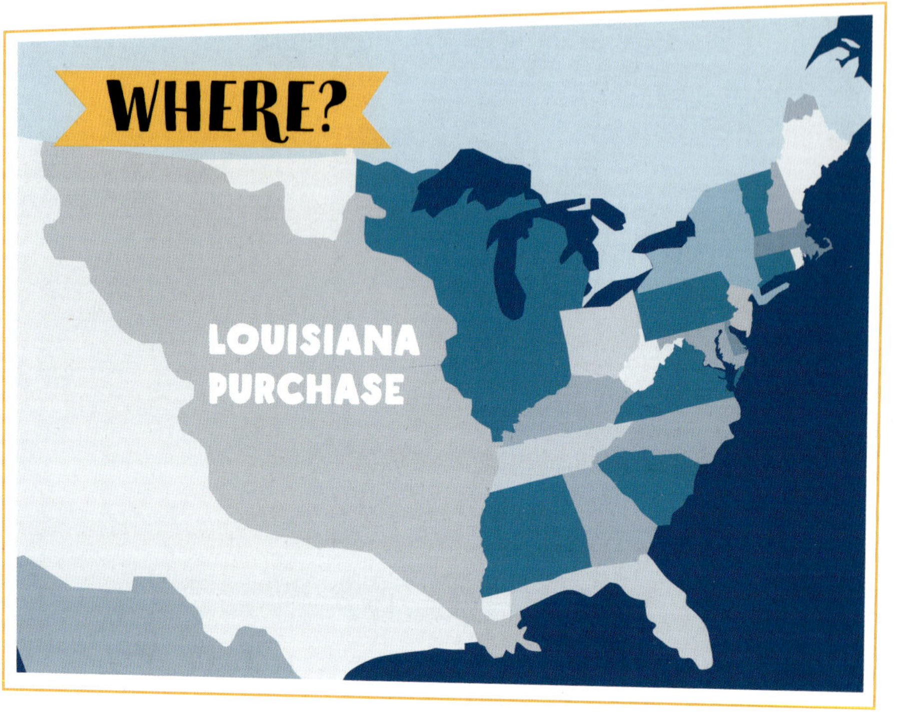

Thomas hired Meriwether Lewis and William Clark to explore the new **territory** and make a map of it. He thought that a route from the East Coast to the West Coast could make trading with Asia faster. If so, the United States would become richer and more powerful. When Lewis and Clark returned, they brought back maps they had drawn and reported on the rivers, land, plants, animals, and indigenous people they had seen.

Thomas was a popular president. With more land and lower taxes, many people felt good about the future. When Thomas ran for president again, he easily won.

The Later Years

After his second term as president, Thomas chose not to run again. He had accomplished many things, including a new slavery law. It ended the sale of enslaved people from other countries into the United States. Thomas knew

JUMP –IN THE– THINK TANK

Thomas helped create a nation, laws, and a college that have lasted for hundreds of years. If you could create something long-lasting, what would it be?

this law would not end slavery, but he hoped it would help it end sooner.

Thomas went home to Monticello to read, write, play music, and think. He had many ideas. He sold 6,487 of his books to Congress to become the nation's library, called the Library of Congress. He also wanted more students to have a better education, so he created a public university. Thomas designed its buildings and planned its classes. The University of Virginia opened in 1825, and it is still strong today.

During **retirement** Thomas and John Adams became friends again. They wrote to each other for many years, about their health, families, and the nation. When they wrote about the past, they sometimes remembered things differently, but they were proud of the work they had done.

> “I cannot **live** without **books.**”

Both Thomas and John were elderly and not in good health. On July 4, 1826, the nation’s 50th birthday, Thomas died shortly after noon. Five hundred miles away, John Adams died on the same day. Each believed the other still lived.

Thomas Jefferson helped shape the United States into the country it is today. His ideas about equality, **liberty**, and democracy helped lead to the rights and freedoms promised to every American today.

WHEN?

1801	Thomas is elected president of the United States.
1803	The Louisiana Purchase is made.
1804	Lewis and Clark explore the new land.
1804	Thomas is elected president for a second term.
1825	Thomas opens the University of Virginia.
1826	Thomas and John Adams both die on July 4.

CHAPTER 8

SO . . . WHO WAS THOMAS JEFFERSON?

Challenge Accepted!

Thomas Jefferson helped create a new nation, the United States of America. Let's test your knowledge of Thomas Jefferson and his legacy in a who, what, when, where, why, and how quiz. Feel free to look back in the text to find the answers if you need to, but try to remember first!

1 Where was Thomas Jefferson born?

- A Massachusetts
- B New York
- C Virginia
- D Connecticut

2 What job did Thomas Jefferson have?

- A Governor of Virginia
- B Ambassador to France
- C President of the United States
- D All the above

3 **What document did Thomas Jefferson write that announced England no longer owned and ruled over the American colonies?**

- A Magna Carta
- B The Declaration of Independence
- C Rights of Man
- D The Gettysburg Address

4 **Who were the two presidents before Thomas Jefferson?**

- A George Washington and John Adams
- B John Adams and Abraham Lincoln
- C George Washington and Abraham Lincoln
- D Alexander Hamilton and George Washington

5 **Thomas Jefferson represented the United States in which country?**

- A China
- B France
- C India
- D Germany

6 **Who helped Thomas Jefferson escape from the Green Dragoons when they went to Monticello to capture him?**

- A George Wythe and George Washington
- B Reverend Douglas and Abraham Lincoln
- C George Washington and John Adams
- D Jack Jouett and Martin Hemings

7 **What did Thomas Jefferson say he could not live without?**

- A Cake
- B Books
- C Conversation
- D Naps

8 **What deal did Thomas Jefferson make with France that doubled the size of the United States and forced native peoples to be removed from land their ancestors had lived on for thousands of years?**

- A Rocky Mountain Agreement
- B Go West Plan
- C Green Acres Expansion
- D The Louisiana Purchase

9 **What is the name of the plantation that Thomas designed and had enslaved people build?**

- A The White House
- B House on the Hill
- C Independence Hall
- D Monticello

10 **What school did Thomas create?**

- A The University of Virginia
- B George Washington University
- C The University of Alexander Hamilton
- D The College of William & Mary

Answers: 1. C, 2. D, 3. B, 4. A, 5. B, 6. D, 7. B, 8. D, 9. D, 10. A

Our World

How has Thomas's work changed our world today? Let's look at a few things that have happened because of Thomas Jefferson's revolutionary ideas.

- → Thomas wrote the Declaration of Independence. This document helped the American colonies break away from England and become a new, independent nation, the United States of America. The Declaration also described many of Thomas's ideas about equality and freedom. These ideas became part of the **Constitution**, a set of instructions that the United States still uses to run the country today.

- → Thomas collected thousands of books for his library at Monticello. When he sold 6,487 books to Congress, they became the foundation for the nation's library, the Library of Congress. It has grown to nearly 25 million books today. You can visit it online at LOC.gov.

- → Thomas taught himself architecture and designed many beautiful buildings and gardens, including the mansion and grounds at Monticello, Virginia's State Capitol building, and the Rotunda at the University of Virginia. These masterpieces were built by enslaved carpenters, artisans, and gardeners, and can be visited today.

JUMP IN THE THINK TANK FOR MORE!

Now let's think a little more about what Thomas Jefferson did, why he did it, and the ways he changed our world.

→ Can you imagine if someone else had written the Declaration of Independence? Do you think the United States would exist without Thomas's revolutionary ideas? What do you think the United States would be like?

→ Thomas read books by the greatest thinkers in the Western world. Some lived when Thomas did, and others lived thousands of years before Thomas. Do you think Thomas would have had the same ideas if he did not read books?

→ Although Thomas wrote that slavery was wrong, and he worked to pass laws that made slavery weaker, he still enslaved 600 people in his lifetime. What do you think might have happened if Thomas had freed his slaves?

Glossary

acre: A measurement of land. One acre is 43,560 square feet.

African: Having to do with the continent of Africa

ambassador: An official representative of a country

ancestors: The relatives a person or group of people descends from

architecture: The art and science of designing physical structures, most often buildings

butler: The most important male servant in a house

cabinet: The group of top government officials who advise the president of the United States

capital: The city where the government of a country or region is located

citizen: A person who legally lives in and belongs to a country or place

college: A school for higher education

colonial: Having to do with a colony

colony: Land that is owned by a country, usually a country that is far away. People who live in a colony are **colonists**. More than one colony is **colonies**.

congress: A formal meeting of delegates; or group of elected people who make laws

Congress: The branch of the United States government that consists of elected people who make laws

conscience: A sense of right or wrong

Constitution: The document written right after the United States became a country that states basic laws, instructions, and rules for how the United States must be run

construction: The act of building something

Declaration of Independence: The 1776 document announcing the American colonies were a separate country, no longer part of England

delegates: People chosen to act for or represent others

democracy: A government ruled by the people either directly or through elected representatives

elect: To pick someone by voting. The process is called an **election**, and the winner is **elected**.

enslaved: Forced to work without the freedom to choose and without pay

enslaved people: People forced into slavery; also known as slaves

equality: When every person in a group has the same rights and opportunities

fascinated: Very interested in something

freedom: The ability to think, speak, and behave as you want without restrictions

government: A system of rules and people that manage a country, state, city, or local community

governor: Leader of a state government or colony

Green Dragoons: A group that fought against George Washington's army during the Revolutionary War

House of Burgesses: A group of people voted into government to make and change laws in the colony of Virginia. The House was created in 1619 and ended in 1776.

indigenous: Original to a place; native

inherited: Got something as a gift from a person when they died

lawyer: A person who has studied the law and can represent other people or groups of people in court

liberty: Freedom

militia: People with some military training ready for emergency service; not part of a country's army

native: Born in a certain place or country

Native Americans: Members of the group of people who lived in America before Europeans arrived, and their descendants

plantation: A large farm or piece of land that uses manual labor to take care of crops and agriculture, such as cotton, tobacco, and sugar, so that they can be sold

planter: The manager or owner of a plantation

practice: In relation to religion, to hold the beliefs of a religion and to participate regularly in its activities

precious: Special or important

president: The elected leader of a country or organization

protest: The act of showing that you disagree with something

quill: A pen made from a bird's feather that is dipped in ink to write

represent: To speak or act for someone officially

representative: A person elected to speak for the people who voted for them

retirement: A time when a person has left their career and is no longer actively working

revolutionary: Having to do with a complete or dramatic change

Revolutionary War: A war from 1775 to 1783 that led to America's independence from England

rights: Legal permission to have certain freedoms or act in certain ways

Second Continental Congress: The American colonies' chosen government from 1775 to 1781

slave: A person forced to give up their freedom and work for no pay in the system called slavery; also known as an enslaved person

slavery: A system in which people are treated like property and forced to work against their will for no pay

surveyor: A person who measures, explores, and writes a report on a piece of land

tax: Money the government collects from its citizens to help pay for things that everyone needs, like schools and roads; more than one are called **taxes**

territory: An area of land that belongs to the government

treason: An act against one's country

tutors: Private teachers who teach students one-on-one or in small groups

university: A college or higher place of learning

vice president: The president's second-in-command, who will take over if the president can't lead anymore

vote: To decide on something officially

wealthy: Rich

Bibliography

Chrysler Museum of Art. Norfolk, Virginia. Chrysler.org.

Colonial Williamsburg. Williamsburg, Virginia. ColonialWilliamsburg.org.

The History Hour. *Thomas Jefferson: Patriot. Statesman. President. The Entire Life Story: Great Biographies*. Read by Jerry Beebe. The History Hour, 2019. Audible audio ed., 1 hr., 43 min.

Hitchens, Christopher. *Thomas Jefferson: Author of America*. New York: HarperCollins, 2009.

Library of Congress. Washington, DC. LOC.gov.

Meacham, Jon. *Thomas Jefferson: The Art of Power*. New York: Random House, 2012.

Monticello. Home of Thomas Jefferson. Charlottesville, Virginia. Monticello.org.

Reese, William S. "The First Hundred Years of Printing in British North America: Printers and Collectors." American Antiquarian Society. Accessed April 10, 2020. AmericanAntiquarian.org/proceedings/44539460.pdf.

Scharff, Virginia. *The Women Jefferson Loved*. New York: HarperCollins, 2010.

The US National Archives and Records Administration. "Founders Online: Correspondence and Other Writings of Six Major Shapers of the United States." Last modified June 2020. Founders.archives.gov.

The White House. WhiteHouse.gov.

Acknowledgments

Thomas Jefferson delivered founding documents that promised freedom, democracy, and equal rights, and helped set up mechanisms for balancing power among three parts of the government. It was revolutionary, but it was also flawed. Thomas Jefferson wrote that Africans were less intelligent than his own European race, but he was schooled in Western history and philosophy and knew little of African history and culture. He also could not have understood the dangers slaves faced by revealing their intelligence. Was this point of view a justification to deny the multiculturalism of the nation, the equality of Africans and African Americans, and the very humanity of the men, women, and children enslaved for hundreds of years? To enslave people and treat them as if they are machines, tools, or farm animals, a society must tell itself that these people are less than human. Most of the men who signed the Declaration of Independence were slaveholders, and slavery is the original flaw in the nation's foundation. Healing from this requires telling the truth. We cannot know the emotional relationship between Sally Hemings and Thomas Jefferson, but together they created one of the nation's first families, a biracial first family.

Thomas Jefferson's Families

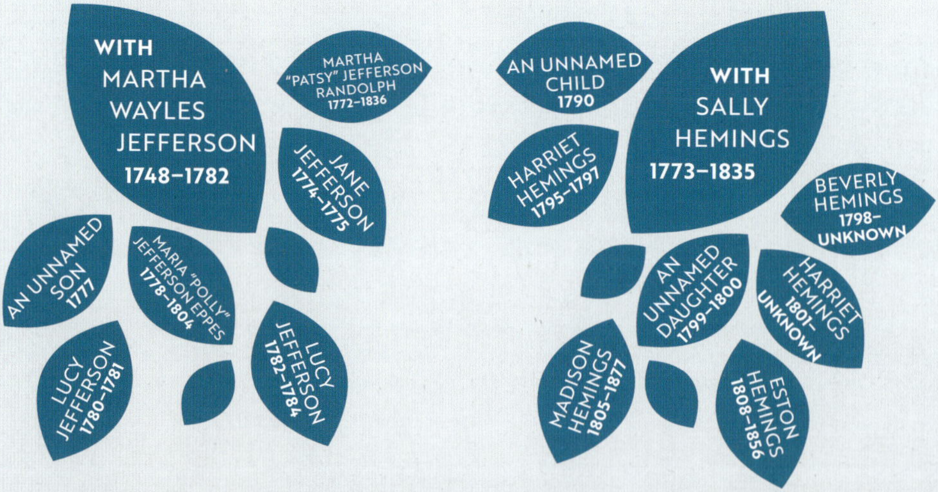

About the Author

LISA TRUSIANI is a writer, artist, advocate, and inventor. Most recently, her book *American Trailblazers: 50 Remarkable People Who Shaped U.S. History* was named the 2019 Lupine Honor Book for juvenile literature by the Maine Library Association. Lisa is happiest writing for children and being with family and friends. She is eternally grateful for Rick, Grant, and Grayson Parker.

About the Illustrator

PATRICK CORRIGAN was born on a crisp, cold December day in a small, cloudy town in Cheshire, England. With a passion for precision as a child, he grew up patiently drawing and designing arts and crafts.

This took him to study ceramics at university, train as an art teacher, and eventually become an art director at a busy design studio where he would work for nearly 10 years. While there, he honed his skills working on more than 500 educational and picture books for children as well as animations and branding.

Now based in Hammersmith, West London—where he lives with his newspaper editor wife, Dulcie, and their fat cat, Forbes—Patrick uses Photoshop, Illustrator, and sometimes even real art equipment to create his work. He draws best when listening to his vast collection of vinyl that he often hides from his wife.

WHO WILL INSPIRE YOU NEXT?

EXPLORE A WORLD OF HEROES AND ROLE MODELS IN ***THE STORY OF***... BIOGRAPHY SERIES FOR NEW READERS.

LOOK FOR THIS SERIES

WHEREVER BOOKS AND EBOOKS ARE SOLD

Alexander Hamilton
Albert Einstein
Martin Luther King Jr.
Ruth Bader Ginsburg
Jane Goodall
Benjamin Franklin
Helen Keller
Marie Curie